Nike: The Origins and History of the Greek Goddess of Victory

By Andrew Scott & Charles River Editors

An ancient carving in Ephesus that depicts Nike

About Charles River Editors

Charles River Editors is a boutique digital publishing company, specializing in bringing history back to life with educational and engaging books on a wide range of topics. Keep up to date with our new and free offerings with this 5 second sign up on our weekly mailing list, and visit Our Kindle Author Page to see other recently published Kindle titles.

We make these books for you and always want to know our readers' opinions, so we encourage you to leave reviews and look forward to publishing new and exciting titles each week.

Introduction

A statuette depicting Nike

Nike

"To Nike (Victory), Fumigation from Manna. O powerful Nike, by men desired, with adverse breasts to dreadful fury fired, thee I invoke, whose might alone can quell contending rage and molestation fell. 'Tis thine in battle to confer the crown, the victor's prize, the mark of sweet renown; for thou rulest all things, Nike divine! And glorious strife, and joyful shouts are thine. Come, mighty goddess, and thy suppliant bless, with sparkling eyes, elated with success; may deeds illustrious thy protection claim, and find, led on by thee, immortal fame." - Orphic Hymn to Nike 33[1]

It seems to be a normal, modern-day practice to reduce all the gods of the ancient pantheons to their most basic abstract concepts: Ares represents war; Demeter, agriculture; Aphrodite, love;

---

[1] Trans. Taylor 1987

and so on. In the process, these characters lose any personality with which they might have been imbued over millennia of stories. A part of most studies of these gods is usually reserved for the undoubtedly valuable etymology of a deity's name, but more often than not, this etymology reveals little more than the fact they had been associated with their abstract concepts since time immemorial.

Take Ares, for example. After the fall of the Mycenaean Civilization (ca.1100 BCE), the word "ares" usually appears fully legible in the archaeological record, but it does not always to refer to the god himself. Homer uses the word "ares" to refer to "battle," and employs it in formulaic expressions, such as "to stand fast against sharp ares" or "to measure one's strength in ares."[2] It appears in the form of an adjective, as well. "Areios" is a fairly common epithet for many gods—such as Zeus Areios or Aphrodite Areios—when referring to their function or appearance in battles and war. Though interesting, such etymology does little more than confirm what is already known of the deity's character from the literary and archaeological record.

Still, most modern readers understand the ancient Greek deities had "personalities" more complex than the abstract concepts they represented. These "personalities" were elaborated upon to explain relationships between concepts, such as in the case of Ares's and Aphrodite's daughter Harmonia, who always followed in her father's destructive wake, explaining the brutal "cleansing" power of war within ancient Greece's complex political landscape. It is in this same line of thought that abstract characters, such as Harmonia and Nike (Victory), find their place in ancient Greek mythology, especially after the writings of Homer in the 8th century BCE. As renowned historian Walter Burkert put it, "as a result of this Homerization, the Archaic Greek personifications come to assume their distinctive character in that they mediate between the individual gods and the spheres of reality, they receive mythical and personal elements from the gods and in turn give the gods part in the conceptual order of things. The personifications appear first in poetry, move into the visual arts and finally find their way into the realm of cult."[3]

In the case of Nike, there is no ambiguity in the meaning of her name. "Nike" is used to refer to the abstract concept of victory in its many forms in the works of Homer, Sophocles, Plato, and Xenophon. Victories in wars and in athletic competitions are invariably Nike's most predominant manifestations in the historical record, and as such, her appearances in myth as a goddess whose actions took place within the society of the pantheon are numerous, though mostly silent. Yet it is how the ancients interacted with this goddess that is most fascinating. The sculpture and the songs, the bas-reliefs and coins, all pay homage to Nike the goddess more intimately than the mere use of her image as a placeholder for "a glorious memory." When viewed in the context of a conversation, the appearance of Nike in the historical and archaeological records give the modern reader a tantalizing view inside the psyche of the ancient Greeks. This is the gift from Nike's that continues to bear fruit.

---

[2] See Burkert 1996
[3] ibid.

Nike: The Origins and History of the Greek Goddess of Victory looks at the story of the legendary deity and the various roles she played in Greek mythology. Along with pictures depicting important people, places, and events, you will learn about Nike like never before.

The Origins of Greek Mythology

"The Titanomachy symbolizes the victory of Order over Chaos." - Niall Livingstone[4]

"the Greek word Mythos can indicate, amongst other things, a public utterance expressing the authority of its speaker."[5] In fact, by the Classical Period, myths were principally instructive, hence Plato's dim view of these stories being in the hands of anyone but philosophers. Myths helped crystallize beliefs and fashion a means of observing and categorizing patterns in daily life. According to Hesiod, the "Pre-World" was populated by personifications;[6] he painted the picture of the primordial geography of his worldview by dramatizing the personification of those elements he considered primal. This is a perfectly arbitrary folkloric trope, but in the case of the ancient Greeks, the antagonism was infused with strains of uncomfortable duality. Hesiod's intention was to glorify Zeus, but in doing so, he created a melodrama that would last the ages.

[4] 2011
[5] Livingstone 2011
[6] Dowden 2011

Marie-Lan Nguyen's picture of a bust of Plato

The "Chasm" mentioned by Hesiod is a synonym for the ancient Greek word for Chaos, and "Earth" is the mighty mother-goddess Gaia, in whom was located the hellish Tartara (or Tartarus), where the Titans would ultimately meet their fate. Interestingly, Hesiod also places Eros, the embodiment of erotic love, at the conception of the cosmos too, thus providing the ancient Greek readers with a foundation for procreation and the lasciviousness of all deities. As a result, the act of creation begins with Chaos, Gaia (Mother Earth), and Eros (Erotic love), but these are no quaint grandparental figures or benign personifications. Chaos was capable of "giving birth" to the most macabre, inherently bleak, and "chaotic" elements of the world, without the need for a reproductive partner.

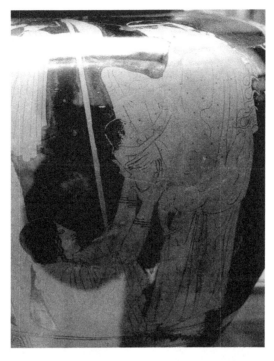

An ancient Greek depiction of Gaia handing her newborn, Erichthonius, to Athena as Hephaestus watches

Chaos spontaneously "bore" both Erebus (Darkness) and Nyx (Night), whose offspring were suitably morbid and must be credited as such in order to lessen the blame on Pandora for "bringing all the sorrow into the world." The list of Nyx's offspring reads like a dreaded guest list of the worst attributes of humanity: the Fates, Death Spirits, Nemesis (Retribution), Apate (Deceit), Geras (Old Age), Eris (Strife), Ponus (Toil), Lethe (Forgetfulness), Limus (Famine), the Algaia (Sorrows), the Hysminae (Fights), the Machae (Battles), the Phonoi (Murders), the Androctasiae (Manslaughters), the Neicea (Quarrels), Pseudea Logoi (Lies) the Amphillogiae (Disputes), Dysnomia (Lawlessness), Ate (Delusion), and finally, as a frail light in the darkness and the law that maintains it, Philotes (Friendship), and Horcus (Oath). It's important to remember these bleak personifications are the inhabitants of the world into which the Titans would be born. From the very beginning of Hesiod's *Theogony*, the reader is greeted with an array of reasons as to why "order" is to be honored and achieved at any cost.

Seeing that Chaos had no need for her, Gaia had to become her own catalyst for the cosmos.

Gaia "bore" Ouranos (Sky), whom Hesiod refers to as "Starry Heaven," so that "he should cover her all about, to be a secure seat for ever for the blessed gods." It wouldn't be long, however, before said "Starry Heaven" had lost all connection with any "security" for the gods or otherwise.

Gaia's incestuous union with her firstborn son would become the most decisive act in the early stages of the Greek cosmological story, but it also set the scene for the discernible world in which the ancient Greeks lived, with a fertile Earth embraced by an all-encompassing Sky. Out of this visible union were born the "insatiably bellicose"[7] Hecatoncheires (the "Hundred-Handed Giants"), the Gigantes (the Giants), as well as the famous one-eyed Cyclopes, who were credited with building those very same "great walls of the palace of Mycenae." The most powerful, first generation beings, whose monstrous power would become pivotal to the war that was to come between the gods and the Titans, are credited with laying the bricks and mortar of this mystical prior power structure. This connection between a real human past and the deeds of the divine is indicative of Hesiod's idea of a "Golden Age," in which humans and divine beings inhabited the same plane of existence and candidly interacted with each other. As this makes clear, even after two centuries of no significant building works, the crumbling walls of ancient palaces still had the power to awe and inspire theories of a divine past.

[7] Vernant 1996a

Johann Heinrich Wilhelm Tischbein's depiction of Polyphemus

Unlike the first generation of Ouranos and Gaia's offspring–not to mention those who simply materialized out of Chaos–the Titans had more ambiguous roles in early mythology. As Kerényi noted, "these titans are a mysterious group; to suggest that they were originally nature-gods is almost meaningless, and the truth is that we have no idea where most of them come from."[8] Unlike their forebears, Hesiod gives the Titans very few ostensibly "personified" names but instead gives them more rounded personalities. Here, the reader can begin to see a progression from chaos to order with every succession of power:

Bedded with Heaven (Ouranos), Gaia bore deep-swirling Oceanus, Koios and Kreios and Hyperion and Iapetos, Thea and Rhea and Themis and Mnemosyne (Memory), Phoebe of gold diadem, and lovely Tethys. After them the youngest was born, crooked schemer Chronos, most fearsome of children, who loathed his lusty father.[9] This is Hesiod's first account of the names of the first 12 Titans. "Deep-swirling Oceanus" refers to the enormous river the Greeks believed encircled their world. Mnemosyne, the Titan of "Memory," would go on to sleep with her nephew, Zeus, and give birth to the famous Muses, those favorites of the poets who inspired Hesiod to write his account. Aside from these two Titans, the names are not personifications, but individualistic. Rather than represent any ubiquitous force or element, their own characters and actions take hold of the story, and the reader is ushered into a new epoch of protagonists and antagonists, especially when it comes to that "crooked schemer," Chronos.

---

[8] 1963
[9] *Theogony Lines 133-138*

A Roman mosaic depicting Ouranos and Gaia

Hesiod refers to the Titans as "chthonic." They were "born of the Earth," and their subsequent "imprisonment" within her defines them even further. Ouranos hated his children, and once born, he forced Gaia to place them back inside her and guard them there indefinitely. Ouranos had no intention of curbing his lust for Gaia–no doubt caused by his primordial uncle Eros–and he "enveloped" her even while she was pregnant, though he would not allow "nature" to come to pass afterward. It's here, in Hesiod's *Theogony*, that the reader gets the first glimpse of an aberration of nature, with a wicked father overpowering a divine mother.

To Ouranos, all those that were born of Earth and Heaven were the most fearsome of children, and their own father loathed them from the beginning. As soon as each of them was born, he hid them all away in a cavern of Earth, and would not let them into the light. He took pleasure in the wicked work, while the huge Earth was tight-pressed inside, and groaned. Finally, she thought up a nasty trick. Without delay, she created the element of grey adamant, made a great reaping hook, and showed it to her dear children and spoke to give them courage, sore at heart as she was: "Children of mine and of an evil father, I wonder whether you would like to do as I say? We could get redress for your father's cruelty. After all, he began it by his ugly behaviour."[10]

This appeal to the Titans to avenge the injustices brought upon them by their wicked father would be echoed by their own offspring, and the "call to arms" would come to symbolize the transition of one power system to another, according to a "natural law of behavior" (since it was the ugliness of Ouranos's behavior that would lead to his downfall). Here, the reader is faced with another common mythological trope: that of creating a tool for one purpose, only to have it used by another, somewhat contradictory purpose later on.

In order to usurp their wicked father, Chronos would use a new element specifically created for the purpose: Adamant. This element would become the metal of choice for the weapons the gods would later wield in their revolt against their own wicked father, the original "adamant-wielder," Chronos. The demise of Ouranos would not only liberate Gaia and the Titans, but would also result in the creation of yet more players in this primordial divine theater.

After Gaia handed Chronos the adamant sickle and explained to him the "stratagem," the defining moment of separation took place: "Great Heaven came, bringing on the night and, desirous of love, he spread himself over Earth, stretched out in every direction. His son reached out from the ambush with his left hand...with his right he took the huge sickle with its long row of sharp teeth and quickly cut off his father's genitals, and flung them behind him to fly where they might."[11]

The Sky was cleaved from Mother Earth, and both she and the Titans were liberated from tyranny. From the conservatively described "drops of blood" were born the Giants "in gleaming armour with long spears in their hands," the nymphs who would occupy the woods and forests of the world and the Erinyes, the so-called "Furies" who would hunt down and punish those perpetrators of the most heinous crimes known to humankind. After he cut off their genitals, Chronos threw them into the sea, where they floated in a "white foam." Out of this foam–or "Aphros" in ancient Greek–sprang forth the first goddess. Just as Eros had been present at the establishment of the first power system, Aphrodite, the more elaborate representative of love and desire, would be present to usher in the next.

---

[10] *Theogony Lines 159-161*
[11] *Lines 170-187*

Sandro Boticelli's painting of the birth of Aphrodite

Peter Paul Rubens" picture of Chronos devouring one of his children

Liberated from their manumission and in the presence of Aphrodite, there came a new surge in reproduction amongst the Titans. A plethora of new deities, rivers, nymphs, and monsters appeared and assumed their roles in the new cosmos, governed by the sons and daughters of that wicked Ouranos. As mentioned earlier, their offspring wasn't inherently wicked, as they included such beings as Helios (the Sun), the Horae (the Seasons), and thousands of wood and sea nymphs. This is worth bearing in mind when considering the role of the Titans as antagonists later on.

After a lengthy description of the unions of the Titans and the fruit they bore, Hesiod turns to the moment where Rhea, "surrendering to (her brother) Chronos, bore resplendent children:" "Hestia, Demeter, and gold-sandaled Hera, mighty Hades who lives under the earth, merciless of heart, and [Poseidon,] the booming Shaker of Earth, and Zeus the resourceful, father of gods and men, under whose thunder the broad earth is shaken."[12]

In typical fashion, Chronos learned from Gaia and Ouranos that it was fated for him to be defeated by his own child (Hesiod doesn't explain when his castrated father gave him this proclamation). Having learned something from his father–namely that Gaia couldn't be trusted to imprison her offspring and they would eventually have to be set free upon the world–Chronos decided to devour his children as they were born. In her suffering, Rhea appealed to her parents–Gaia and Ouranos–for a stratagem to save her children from this fate. Gaia told her to go to a town called Lyktos in Crete to give birth. When she did, Gaia accepted the youngest god, Zeus, into a mountain on that fateful island and wrapped a stone in "babycloth" to give to his voracious father in lieu of the child. Chronos swallowed the stone without so much as a sneaking suspicion he was about to be overthrown, like his father had been before him.

---

[12] *Lines 454-460*

An illustration depicting Rhea giving the stone to Chronos

Chronos regurgitated each god in reverse order, the stone coming first and falling at Delphi, where it was venerated thenceforth. With this "re-birth" of the gods, the scene was set for a cataclysmic confrontation and an apocalyptic power struggle. Vengeance had to be exacted for the rape of their mother and their own imprisonment. The first twelve Titans had given birth to most of the ubiquitous elements of the cosmos. Not only did this create the backdrop for a new order of rule, but it was also the fertile ground from which all stories–mythological and factual–could grow and be imbued with meaning, according to the cosmological order.

The "titanomachy"–the war wreaked upon the Titans–was a defining moment in the evolution of Greek mythological thought. It was the moment where the Greeks developed a "greater self-awareness of their own social life and thought"[13] in the face of the "barbaric other," and it was so

---

[13] 1984

much more than a fight of "good versus evil," as is often thought to be the case.

The term "titanomachy" is a compound word, incorporating "titan" and the Greek word "Machia," meaning "fight" or "battle." Just like the Amazonomachy (battle against the fearsome Amazons) and the Centauromachy (battle against the Centaurs), the Titanomachy was depicted in the metopes of the Parthenon in Athens. The scenes selected for the metopes were those depicting quintessential "battles against the other." The Parthenon was a monument erected in the wake of the Persian Wars, the biggest, most cataclysmic invasion the Greeks had suffered in 700 years. Although this was a fight against "the other," it was a defining moment in ancient Greek history and of the mind-set of that peculiar collective. Their relatively young power systems had faced seemingly insurmountable odds against an older kingdom and had survived victorious, quashing chaos and constructing order from the rubble.

Cornelis Cornelisz van Haarlem's "The Fall of the Titans"

Joachim Wtewael's "The Battle Between the Gods and the Titans"

A depiction of Zeus launching a thunderbolt on the Temple of Artemis at Corfu

Although the epic poets Homer and Hesiod "attributed to the divine powers everything that is harmful and blameworthy in men: stealing, committing adultery and deceiving one another,"[14] the Titans were depicted as something worse, embodying the rule of disorder and hubris. Although the gods were fallible and innately "human" in their vices, they were ultimately progressive. The Titans were "chthonic," representing "Nature" in the battle against the more "cultured"–and certainly, more elaborate–personalities of the Olympian gods, who in this episode, are representative of order and culture.

Ultimately, the Titanomachy is a classic story of the revolt[15] of the new against the old, culture against nature, and order against chaos. It is a story indicative of a people who have undergone multiple power struggles and states of unrest. As is the case with most cultures, the ancient Greeks defined their contemporary state of existence by the series of "boundary catastrophes" that had preceded it.[16] For that reason, the Titanomachy wasn't just another piece of "art as propaganda," but instead a defining moment in ancient Greek culture.

The Myths

Nike's parentage, like many anthropomorphised concepts, is not always consistent. There are two "schools" of source material on the matter. In the Homeric Hymn to Ares (4), possibly written as early as the 7th century BCE, the writer gives Nike a short but easily supposed patronage: "[Ares] father of warlike (eupolemos) Nike, ally of Themis."[17] Here, the Greek term "eupolemos" is an adjective with a meaning closer to "good or skilful at war" than the notions of "belligerence" or "bellicose" conjured by the term "warlike."[18] Of course, the goddess of "victory" is still very likely to be associated with the god of "war" in any circumstance. The ubiquity and regularity of war—the warmer months were the accepted "campaigning season"— necessitated the creation of a deity that was able to bestow a victory.

On the other hand, there is a curious fact about this source that must be taken into consideration: it is the only one that depicts Nike as a daughter of Ares. Given the fact that the Homeric Hymns are of great antiquity, they are often referred to as authorities on the lives and genealogies of the gods, but in this case, it is alone in its assertion of Ares' fatherhood. The Homeric writer makes no mention of Nike's divine mother, either, making this provenance more of a parentage of logical association than any kind of elaborated myth. On the other hand, there are at least four other noteworthy sources claiming Nike to be the daughter of Pallas and Styx.

"And Styx the daughter of Okeanos (Oceanus) was joined to Pallas and bore Zelos (Emulation)

---

[14] Vernant 1983
[15] Detienne 1981
[16] Breton Connelly 2014
[17] Evelyn-White 1914
[18] Liddel & Scott 1940

and trim-ankled Nike (Victory) in the house. Also she brought forth Kratos (Cratus, Strength) and Bia (Force), wonderful children."[19] This quote, from Hesiod's *Theogony*, written in the 8th century BCE, outlines the most common and generally accepted of Nike's genealogies. The father of emulation, victory, strength, and force (referring to both physical and mental strength) was not Ares, but the Titan Pallas. Pallas's name comes from the Greek "to wield/brandish a spear," and so he was considered the "Titan of War Craft." Nike's origins, then, are never far from the sphere of war, but in subsequent myths, she is increasingly aligned with the war-goddess Athena than her own father, a fact that would come to shape the mental and physical landscape of the ancient Greeks for years to come.

Her mother, Styx, was both goddess and the dreaded river finding its source in the land of the living, but which had to be crossed by the boatman, Charon, in the Land of the Dead. Styx's attributes as a river present some interesting connections with her daughter. Firstly, her waters were said to give the gift of corporeal invincibility. It was into this river the nymph Thetis dipped her child, Achilles, after hearing war would bring immortality to his name, but would also cut his mortal life drastically short. Every part of the child's body the water touched became impervious to harm, but the heel from which she held him would become the most famous weakness the world would ever know.

Achilles was not only the protagonist of Homer's *Iliad*. Often referred to as "The Wrath of Achilles," he was the embodiment of the perfect Homeric warrior. His absence on the battlefield was apropos to the absence of Nike. When Achilles was insulted by Agamemnon, the leader of the Greeks who had taken took Achilles's "prize spoil of war," and chose not to leave his tent, the tide of the decade-long war took a swift turn. The Greeks were eventually beaten back from Troy's walls and forced to fight among their own ships on the beach. 10 years of advancement toward the enemy city, of meeting the Trojans as equals in battle, and taking their share of the victory were done away with in a moment when the blessing of the Styx was taken away from the war.

This connection to Nike as a "war-goddess" became further established thanks to Styx's role in the Titanomachy. After the Titans elected the great Atlas as their leader and Zeus agreed to lead the gods, he called out to all the beings in existence to come to his aid. "For so did Styx the deathless daughter of Okeanos plan on that day when the Olympian Lightener called all the deathless gods to great Olympos (Olympus), and said that whosoever of the gods would fight with him against the Titanes (Titans), he would not cast him out from his rights, but each should have the office which he had before amongst the deathless gods. And he declared that he who was without office and rights as is just. So deathless Styx came first to Olympos with her children through the wit of her dear father. And Zeus honoured her, and gave her very great gifts, for her he appointed to be the great oath of the gods, and her children to live with him always. And as he promised, so he performed fully unto them all."[20] In this telling of the myth, Styx is

---

[19] Hesiod *Theogony 383ff*

the first to come to Zeus' aid and she brings her children with her. By "be the great oath of the gods," it is meant that it was in her name and upon the name of "her waters" that the all the gods—including Zeus and his wife, Hera—henceforth swore their oaths. "[Hera addresses Zeus:] "Now let Gaia (Gaea, Earth) be my witness in this, and wide Ouranos (Uranus, Heaven) above us, and the dripping water of the Styx, which oath is the biggest and most formidable oath among the blessed immortals.""[21]

Zeus adopts both Kratos (power) and Zelus (emulation or zeal) to be the attendants of his throne, and in doing so, he "adopts" the qualities of the future ruler of the cosmos. To Nike, he entrusts the driving of his chariot. Far from a glorified chauffeur, drivers of chariots were highly respected at the time of Homer's writing.

Throughout the *Iliad*, chariot warfare was considered the domain of the aristocracy, the "high-powers" whose rule was a matter of cosmic order. By entrusting his chariot to Nike, Zeus travels with "Victory," thus assimilating her abstract qualities on a cosmic scale. Nike does not "bestow her gifts" on Zeus as she does mortal men. Instead, she offers herself as a permanent companion, and in doing so, she and her siblings affirm Zeus' right to the throne of Mt. Olympos.

Nike's father, Pallas, also appears in this episode, but since he, too, was a Titan, he fights against Zeus with disastrous consequences. Pallas's last battle was to be against Athena—the goddess of war and wisdom outwitted her opponent with stratagem, and as any good warrior would, took from him two crucial spoils of war. [In the War of the Gigantes/Titans: Athena] stripped the skin off Pallas and used it to protect her own body during the battle.[22]

As tradition has it, Athena took Pallas's skin to Hephaestus' volcanic forge, where he crafted the famous Aegis, which Athena and Zeus bore into battle. This was considered a sign of superior force on the battlefield, and anybody who came "under" it in their actions could depend upon the protection of Athena, Zeus, or both. Hence the modern phrase, "to do something under somebody's aegis." "Pallas: A great virgin. It is an epithet of Athena; from brandishing (pallein) the spear, or from having killed Pallas, one of the Gigantes (Giants)."[23]

As a second spoil of war, Athena took Pallas's name and adopted it as an epithet of her own. This is a powerfully symbolic action in terms of the evolution of Nike's character. Not only does Athena defeat Nike's father—the incumbent Titan of Athena's would-be domain—she appropriates his very essence as a divine being. This is similar to the manner in which Zeus appropriated Athena's mother, Metis', "cunning" or "resourcefulness" by swallowing her. According to Liddell and Scott's Lexicon, "Pallas" could also be defined as "youth," but when Athena appropriated it as an epithet, the connection to her defeated foe was diminished. The

---

[20] Hesiod *Theogony 386ff*
[21] Homer *Iliad 15.35*
[22] Pseudo-Apollodorus *Bibliotheca 1. 38*
[23] *Suidas s.v. Pallas*

epithet then took on the meaning of "virgin," one of her primary characteristics as a goddess.

Nike also played a crucial role in the battle against Typhon, the largest beast ever conceived. His appearance was no less daunting. They say that, from the waist down, he was a mess of coiled and writhing serpents, and instead of hands, his enormous arms were tipped with countless serpent heads. His head reached the stars, and his eldritch wings darkened the sun's majesty. He was an abomination born of rage and singular purpose.[24] [When the monster Typhoeus (Typhon) besieged Olympos (Olympus), all the gods fled except for Zeus and Nike:] Zeus was alone, when Nike (Victory) came to comfort him, scoring the high paths of the air with her shoe. She had the form of Leto; and while she armed her father, she made him a speech full of reproaches with guileful lips. "Lord Zeus! Stand up as champion of your own children! Let me never see Athena mingled with Typhon [Typhoeus], she who knows not the way of a man with a maid! Make not a mother of the unmothered! Fight, brandish your lightning, the fiery spear of Olympos! Gather once more your clouds, lord of the rain! For the foundations of the steadfast universe are already shaking under Typhon's hands: the four blended elements are melted! Deo [Demeter] has renounced her harvests. Hebe has left her cup, Ares has thrown down his spear, Hermes has dropped his staff, Apollon has cast away his harp, and taken a swan's form, and flown off on the wing, leaving his winged arrows behind! Aphrodite, the goddess who brings wedlock to pass, has gone a wandering, and the universe is without seed. The bonds indissoluble of harmony are dissolved, leaving behind his generative arrows, the adorner of brides, he the all-mastering, the unmastered! And your fiery Hephaistos (Hephaestus) has left his favourite Lemnos, and dragging unruly knees, look how slowly he keeps his unsteady course! See a great miracle—I pity your Hera, though she hates me sure enough! What—is your begetter [Kronos (Cronus)] to come back into the assembly of the stars? May that never be, I pray! Even if I am called a Titenis, I wish to see no Titan lords of Olympos, but you and your children. Take your lordly thunderbolt and champion chaste Artemis."[25]

Although her words seemed to come from Leto, Nike's rousing words were unmistakable and unfailing. Zeus picked up his thunderbolts and led the charge back to Mount Olympus. He threw himself at the mighty beast and was bested again and again. But when the gods saw their leader battle Typhon, they returned, en masse. It was with their help Zeus eventually slew the monster atop Mt. Haemus, which got its name from the torrents of black blood flowing down it on that day from the defeated beast's corpse.[26]

It would seem, then, Nike, when she isn't imparting victory by her very presence, can upbraid even the gods when she feels they aren't seizing the opportunities they have been given. She was one of the first to join Zeus's cause, and she was not about to let him and the other gods abandon their hard-won prize just because defeat seemed certain. It is under exactly those circumstances

[24] See Graves 1955
[25] Nonnus *Dionysiaca 2. 205 ff*
[26] See Graves 1955

that victory may be snatched from the maw of even the most dreaded monster, such as Typhon.

Nike's Presence

A visit to the Louvre Museum in Paris is replete with epiphanic encounters with masterpieces. The 20th century pyramid nestled into its palatial abode on the right bank of the River Seine is a crystalline beacon announcing the treasures within. In 1883, a young French vice-consul to the government of Adrianople arrived on the small island of Samothrace in the northern Aegean, keen on exploring the ruins he had heard so much about. Little did he know, he was about to add to the Louvre's treasures in a way he never could have imagined.

At this time, it was customary for young travelers from Northern Europe to wander southward to "rediscover" the classical civilizations by exploring ruins and purloining certain artifacts every now and again. More often than not, these artifacts swapped the public sphere for the private, as they were spirited away to join the many private collections throughout Europe and abroad. In his capacity as temporary vice-consul, however, Charles Champoiseau scoured the ruins of Samothrace for some pieces for the Imperial French Museum in Paris. An avid amateur archaeologist, Champoiseau hired a team of workers and began excavating a site he believed to be an antiquarian gold mine, and he was not wrong. When the marble feathers and billowy folds of Nike's dress emerged from the detritus, Champoiseau knew he had found a piece to rival all others in the museum. The 2.44m Nike, wings spread out behind her, now occupies the principal position on the Daru staircase in the Louvre, welcoming guests to the collections with fanfare. And yet, her original *situ* was perhaps even more extravagant still.

Nathanael Burton's picture of the statue

I. Sailko's picture of the statue before restoration

The Daru staircase with the statue in the background

Champoiseau traveled to the north of the island, where there is a curious, naturally formed gully carved into the foot of the mountain, also the home of the "Temple Complex of the Great Gods" (Kabeiroi/Megaloi Theoi). This was one of the great "Pan-Hellenic" sanctuaries—like Delphi and Olympia—to which all Greeks were invited to partake in the worship performed there.

A picture of the ruins of the temple complex

Furthermore, Samothrace was the site of another great mystery religion, similar to that of Athenian Eleusis, an adept who was none other than the "Father of History," Herodotus. Writing at some time in the 5th century BCE, Herodotus described the original inhabitants of Samothrace, the Pelasgians, and hints at what was revealed to him when he became an initiate of the mysteries there.

"For the Athenians were then already counted as Greeks when the Pelasgians came to live in the land with them and thereby began to be considered as Greeks. Whoever has been initiated into the rites of the Cabeiri (Kabeiri), which the Samothracians learned from the Pelasgians and now practice, understands what my meaning is. Samothrace was formerly inhabited by those Pelasgians who came to live among the Athenians, and it is from them that the Samothracians take their rites. The Athenians, then, were the first Greeks to make ithyphallic images of Hermes, and they did this because the Pelasgians taught them. The Pelasgians told a certain sacred tale about this, which is set forth in the Samothracian mysteries.

"Formerly, in all their sacrifices, the Pelasgians called upon gods without giving name or appellation to any (I know this, because I was told at Dodona); for as yet

they had not heard of such. They called them gods from the fact that, besides
setting everything in order, they maintained all the dispositions. Then, after a long
while, first they learned the names of the rest of the gods, which came to them
from Egypt, and, much later, the name of Dionysus; and presently they asked the
oracle at Dodona about the names; for this place of divination, held to be the most
ancient in Hellas, was at that time the only one. When the Pelasgians, then, asked
at Dodona whether they should adopt the names that had come from foreign parts,
the oracle told them to use the names. From that time onwards they used the
names of the gods in their sacrifices; and the Greeks received these later from the
Pelasgians."[27]

Herodotus does not reveal much about the mysteries there, of course. Although the
Samothracian mysteries were open to any visitor regardless of gender, age, or civic status, what
was revealed to the initiates was only ever alluded to in public. No initiate ever betrayed the
revelation, though some interesting facts can still be gleaned from this passage. Firstly, there is
the name of the gods worshipped there, the Kabeiri. This word did not have a Greek origin—it
was Pelasgian, as Herodotus has said—and it represented the "great gods" that were worshipped
there.[28] There is reason to believe that, despite the fact they "learned the names of the gods" later,
those names were not used in the rites at Samothrace. The Kabeiri came to be a euphemistic term
for the gods whose names were so sacrosanct, they dare not be spoken, such as YHWH in the
Jewish tradition.[29]

What is known about the Samothracian mysteries is that they were believed to be a successful
way of propitiating the gods to ensure safe maritime travel. This tradition finds its way to the
modern reader in the tale of *Jason and the Argonauts*; Jason and the Argonauts visited the island
of Samothrace for the express purpose of evading shipwreck on their perilous journey to collect
the Golden Fleece. Despite their apparent ambiguity, the great gods attracted enough visitors to
the site—presumably potential initiates as well as seafarers—to warrant the building of an
enormous temple complex there.[30]

When Champoiseau discovered Nike there, he believed she had fallen onto a kind of tomb, as
there were great interlocking stone slabs beneath her, and so he took the statue and left the
"tomb" undisturbed. Thanks to the efforts of Austrian archaeologists digging there after
Champoiseau left, the "tomb" was eventually revealed to be a mock ship upon which Nike was
believed to have stood. Champoiseau immediately arranged for the slabs to be transported to
Paris once he'd learned of this discovery, and viewers today can finally see Nike alighting the
ship's prow in all her glory.

---

[27] Hdt. *Histories* 2.51-52
[28] Graves 1955
[29] Burkert 1996
[30] Colavito 2014

The statue was no doubt a dedication of some kind, and most historians believe it to have commemorated a naval battle. The outstretched wings and the way the ripples in her clothes billow suggests the statue was intended to elicit the exact moment in which Nike touched down on the prow of a victorious battleship. It was common practice to dedicate a statue to a god or goddess in thanks for a victory, and in fact, it was often the ransom or sale into slavery of prisoners captured in said battle that funded the construction of the statue.[31]

There's still a debate over which battle it was intended to commemorate. What is known about the statue is that it was constructed during the Hellenic Period (5th-4th century BCE), but battles as disparate in time as the Battle of Salamis to Octavian's final battle against Mark Antony and Cleopatra at Actium in 31 BCE have been suggested as possible events for the dedication.

Conversely, a recent study has suggested that it was possibly dedicated to commemorate the lesser-known invasion attempt on Pergamon by Prousias II of Bithynia.[32] It was said that Prousias II attempted an invasion of the great city of Pergamon, on what would be the modern-day Turkish coast, in 155 BCE. As is usually the case when reading reports of the losing side, Prousias's men were a marauding mass of sacrilegious barbarians. It is said that on his way from

---

[31] Burkert 1996
[32] Steward 2016

his home in Bithynia, a place in northern Turkey, Prousias sailed his fleet down the coast, raiding and sacking every sanctuary along the way. Considering the old dictum "history is written by the winners," this kind of description doesn't reveal much about Prousias, even if it is true. What it does reveal is the viewpoint of the writer, and just as the writer had an agenda when writing about Prousias, so, too, did the sculptor and sanctuary official who had placed Nike's statue in that setting, since Prousias's entire fleet was said to have been dashed against the rocks by a sudden storm at sea.

If this was truly the reason for the dedication of Nike's statue at Samothrace, then the modern reader is confronted with an excellent example of the duplicity of religious thought. At a sanctuary where sailors propitiated the gods not to dash them against the rocks, those same sailors would thank the gods for dashing their enemies against them, instead. Such is the religious discourse between gods and humans. In the case of ancient Greece, there is a reciprocal gift-exchange, too, in offering a sacrifice for calm seas and favourable winds. Nike chooses onto which noble prow she will land, and the best a human can do is to eschew hubris and impiety and burn the bones and fat of their best animal on her altar.

Nike's presence often has this element of "arrival" associated with it. Just as her following her mother to Zeus's side, and when she appears as the last remaining goddess who chides Zeus for fearing Typhon, Nike invariably appears at the right moment, often with a message to bear and a trumpet with which to announce it. In fact, from the fragments that have survived of her hands, there is evidence to suggest the enormous statue of Nike at Samothrace once held a trumpet or cupped her hand to her mouth to announce her message of victory. This aspect of Nike as a messenger was as common a trait of hers as her outstretched wings or long, flowing robes. Looking at this role of Nike's reveals a connection between ancient Greek divine messengers and those of medieval European religious thought when one considers the ancient Greek word for messenger was *angelos*, or "angel."

The First Persian War of 492-490 BCE brought the Greeks into contact with the largest military force they had met to date. Under the rule of King Darius I, the Persians—or "Medes," since the ancient Greeks rarely distinguished between the two—set out to punish Athens for supporting the revolt of the cities of Ionia against their Persian masters. The Athenians appealed to the Greek states to help them defend their lands against the Persians, forming the first large-scale alliance of the Greek city-states, or *Poleis*. Even still, the Persians often outnumbered the Greeks with daunting odds, which included the final battle of the war at Marathon, a little more than 25 miles northeast of Athens.

By all accounts, the Athenians and their allied Plataeans numbered around 10,000 and their opposition nearly twice that amount.[33] The Athenians appealed to Sparta to come to their aid, but the Spartans were, above all else, devoutly religious, and their forces were not allowed to march

---

[33] Orrieux & Pantel 1995

until after they had taken part in a religious festival happening at the time. As a result, Athens and the Plataeans marched to Marathon heavily outnumbered and having little hope of success against the Persian force. Herodotus documented the Persian Invasions in his *Histories,* and he described the pivotal battle of Marathon as follows:

"The Athenian generals were of divided opinion, some advocating not fighting because they were too few to attack the army of the Medes; others, including Miltiades, advocating fighting. Thus they were at odds, and the inferior plan prevailed. An eleventh man had a vote, chosen by lot to be polemarch of Athens, and by ancient custom the Athenians had made his vote of equal weight with the generals. Callimachus of Aphidnae was polemarch at this time. Miltiades approached him and said, "Callimachus, it is now in your hands to enslave Athens or make her free, and thereby leave behind for all posterity a memorial such as not even Harmodius and Aristogeiton left. Now the Athenians have come to their greatest danger since they first came into being, and, if we surrender, it is clear what we will suffer when handed over to Hippias. But if the city prevails, it will take first place among Hellenic cities... If we do not attack now, I expect that great strife will fall upon and shake the spirit of the Athenians, leading them to Medize. But if we attack now, before anything unsound corrupts the Athenians, we can win the battle, if the gods are fair. All this concerns and depends on you in this way: if you vote with me, your country will be free and your city the first in Hellas. But if you side with those eager to avoid battle, you will have the opposite to all the good things I enumerated."

"[Callimachus voted to fight and the generals deployed at Marathon,] with the polemarch Callimachus commanding the right wing, since it was then the Athenian custom for the polemarch to hold the right wing. He led, and the other tribes were numbered out in succession next to each other. The Plataeans were marshalled last, holding the left wing. Ever since that battle, when the Athenians are conducting sacrifices at the festivals every fourth year, the Athenian herald prays for good things for the Athenians and Plataeans together. As the Athenians were marshalled at Marathon, it happened that their line of battle was as long as the line of the Medes. The centre, where the line was weakest, was only a few ranks deep, but each wing was strong in numbers.

"When they had been set in order and the sacrifices were favourable, the Athenians were sent forth and charged the foreigners at a run...The Persians saw them running to attack and prepared to receive them, thinking the Athenians absolutely crazy, since they saw how few of them there were and that they ran up so fast without either cavalry or archers. So the foreigners imagined, but when the Athenians all-together fell upon the foreigners they fought in a way worthy of record…

"They fought a long time at Marathon. In the centre of the line the foreigners prevailed, where the Persians and Sacae were arrayed. The foreigners prevailed there and broke through in pursuit inland, but on each wing the Athenians and Plataeans prevailed. In victory they let the routed foreigners flee, and brought the wings together to fight those who had broken through the centre. The Athenians prevailed, then followed the fleeing Persians and struck them down. When they reached the sea they demanded fire and laid hold of the Persian ships.

"In this labour Callimachus the polemarch was slain, a brave man, and of the generals Stesilaus son of Thrasylaus died. Cynegirus[1] son of Euphorion fell there, his hand cut off with an axe as he grabbed a ship's figurehead. Many other famous Athenians also fell there."[34]

Although Herodotus called his works *The Histories*, there is a common caveat to which historians refer when considering the veracity of what he wrote, namely that Herodotus never let the facts get in the way of a good story. However, in the case of the polemarch Callimachus (polemarch being a Greek term made up of the words "Polemos," referring to war or battle, and "archon," meaning leader Plataeans), there is an excellent archaeological example corroborating at least some part of Herodotus's story of Marathon.

The Nike of Callimachus (or Kallimachos) is a 4.68 m marble construction, including a "running" Nike atop a tall Ionic column. Although not much of the statue survives today, it is still a very important archaeological find because it contains a large part of the dedicatory inscription carved into the column. The classical historian, Catharine Keesling, translated the two-line inscription as follows:

"[Kallimachos] of Aphidna [de]dicated [me] to Athena,

me[ssenger of the imm]ortals who have [homes on] Olympus

[Kallimachos the pole]march of the Athenians, who fought the battle

at Ma[rathon for the H]ellenes (Greeks),

by/for the children of the Athenians, a memorial…"[35]

The practice of referring to a dedication in the first person ("me") was not uncommon on ancient Greek sculpture or pottery, but the rest of the information on the column is very important, indeed. Knowing who the polemarch of Marathon was, as well as the fact he had

---

[34] Hdt. *Histories* 6.102-110
[35] See Keesling 2010

come from the Attic region (*deme*) of Aphidna, verifies Herodotus's story in a way that few historical events from that period of time can.

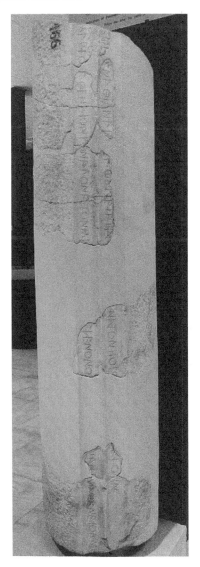

Part of the inscribed column

In 480 BCE, the Persians returned and were successful in their assault on Athens. They marched straight up to the Acropolis and set it ablaze, and the fire destroyed countless artistic masterpieces on the Acropolis, including the Nike of Callimachus, erected there after the Battle of Marathon. Given the potential damage that could have been inflicted, the fact that modern readers are still able to discern the dedication on the column is truly incredible.

Furthermore, it places Nike at another pivotal moment in ancient Greek history, linking her to the Athenian Acropolis, a religious area with surprisingly strong connections to the winged messenger. "There is but one entry to the Acropolis. It affords no other, being precipitous throughout and having a strong wall. The gateway has a roof of white marble, and down to the present day it is unrivalled for the beauty and size of its stones. Now as to the statues of the horsemen, I cannot tell for certain whether they are the sons of Xenophon or whether they were made merely to beautify the place. On the right of the gateway is a temple of Wingless Victory. From this point the sea is visible, and here it was that, according to legend, Aegeus threw himself down to his death."[36] Pausanias was a writer and traveler from Greece who wrote his *Description of Greece* at some time during the 2nd century CE. Pausanias traveled around Greece, setting for himself the task of documenting the state of the cities (*poleis*) and the art and architecture they contained at the time of his writing. This document is remarkably useful for the modern historian because many of the artifacts, and often the buildings, have been lost over the years, so Pausanias remains as one of the few to have documented their existence.

As for the "Temple of Wingless Victory" mentioned in the above quote, the building has survived, though the date of its construction is interesting. Built in 424 BCE, the version that stands today is not the first incarnation of a temple to Nike on the Acropolis. In the Mycenaean period (1600-1100 BCE), the political landscape of Greece was similar to that of later Classical Greece (5th-4th century BCE), except the poleis had a central palace structure with, invariably, a king as the absolute monarch. Beneath the 5th century "Temple of Wingless Victory" are the remnants of a Mycenaean temple to Nike, so her presence on the Acropolis can be traced back to at least this period. During the Second Persian Invasion, this temple suffered the same fate as many of the others in the Persians' fiery wake, but out of the flames, the Acropolis was about to be reborn into the iconic, rocky outcrop of today.

By 478 BCE, the Athenians and their allies had successfully expelled the Persians twice from their lands, but they lived under the constant threat of an even stronger return force, able to subdue them to Persian rule. However, this never came to pass, thanks to the Delian League, an alliance of, according to some records, over 300 *poleis* led by Athens, which kept a constant guard for any sign of a Persian attack. As a part of their alliance, an annual tribute was paid by each member in the form of soldiers, ships, money, or all of the above. The treasury was kept on

---

[36] Pausanias 1.22.4

the small island in the Cyclades, giving the alliance the name of Delos. Once the threat of a Persian invasion became less credible, the Athenians removed the treasury from Delos, re-housing it in Athens. The "allies" of the Delian League fell quickly to the category of "vassal state" in what would become an "Athenian Empire" of sorts.

This influx of money, combined with the charisma of the new Athenian leader, Pericles, led to what came to be known as Athens' "Golden Age." Social reforms that benefitted the poor, governmental re-shuffling that made democracy fairer across the citizenry, and a new refined monetary system coined out of the coffers of the (former) Delian League were all products of this "Golden Age."

A bust of Pericles

Atop the Acropolis—named as such because it was the highest point in the city—Pericles set out to make the most extravagant religious complex ever to have existed in the ancient world, with Nike taking pride of place there. As Pausanias mentioned, the "Temple of Wingless Nike" occupied the space to the right of the extravagant doorway to the Acropolis, known as the Propylaea, and was, itself, an important monument built during this period, with "victory" greeting the faithful whenever they scaled the precipice. Though it was the temple to Athena, the Parthenon, that was considered the prize jewel in the crown of the Acropolis, Nike was nevertheless given a place of honor. "The statue of Athena [inside the Parthenon] is upright, with a tunic reaching to the feet, and on her breast the head of Medusa is worked in ivory. She holds a statue of Victory [Nike] about four cubits high, and in the other hand a spear; at her feet lies a shield and near the spear is a serpent. This serpent would be Erichthonius. On the pedestal is the birth of Pandora in relief. Hesiod and others have sung how this Pandora was the first woman; before Pandora was born there was as yet no womankind."[37]

On the Acropolis, at least, Nike was as inseparable from Athena as the Aegis or the Owl. The statue of Athena was an assemblage of everything within the Athenian worldview. Erichthonius, or Erechtheus, the autochthonic king of Athens who was born after Hephaestus' unwelcome ejaculate was wiped from Athena's thigh and flung to the Earth, appears in the form of the serpent. This serpent was said to be real and living in the Erechtheion temple on the Acropolis, where it was believed the soiled rag landed after Athena tossed it aside in disgust.[38] The frieze of Pandora would have been one of many in the Acropolis. Had it survived, perhaps it would have rivaled the others for their beauty but not for their political weight.

The Acropolis, built on the back of Athens' most noteworthy military and political achievements in living history, was both a religious complex and a political statement. It cemented Athens' place as the leader of a new empire looking forward. Looking back, it recalled her glories. Each of the four sides of the Acropolis housing Athena Nike, as she came to be known, were four series of metopes—slabs of stone with relief carvings on them—each of them designed with the glorification of Athens in mind. To the north, the Trojan War played out along 32 separate relief panels. To the south, the same number of panels showed the fight between the Centaurs and the Lapiths. On the east side, the story of the Gigantomachy was told in 14 panels, and on the west, 14 scenes of the legendary invasion of Athens by those fierce warrior women, the Amazons.

Each of these scenes may appear to be simple fireside stories told by mythmakers in the 5th century but that would be downplaying the power of myth. In each story there is a barbaric "other" whom the "Greeks" defeated. The Trojans were hubristic wife thieves with strange foreign customs; the centaurs could not drink and maintain "propriety" at a wedding; the Giants were arrogant pretenders to a throne that was not theirs by "right;" and the Amazons offended every sensibility the Athenians had concerning the "correct behaviour of a woman." As if the worried message was not clear enough, the artists invariably depicted the "others" wearing an

[37] Pausanias 1.24.7
[38] Burkert 1996

eastern style of dress, particularly the Amazons. All sides of the Parthenon thus "point" to Persia. The ransom of prisoners and the "assimilation" of the Delian League's coffers paid for the temple complex, designed to glorify the Athenian victory over the Persians as much as the gods for being gods, which may explain why this temple at the entrance to the Acropolis featured Nike without wings.

Dimboukas' picture of the Temple of Athena Nike on the Acropolis

In his wanderings through ancient Greece, Pausanias also included his findings of Sparta's architecture and statues. It was there that he noticed an interesting similarity between the two cities that would eventually come to blows in the Peloponnesian War at the end of the 5th century BCE.[39] "Opposite this temple is an old image of Enyalios in fetters. The idea the Lacedaemonians express by this image is the same as the Athenians express by their Wingless Victory; the former think that Enyalios will never run away from them, being bound in the fetters, while the Athenians think that Victory, having no wings, will always remain where she is."[40] Such an act may seem hubristic to the modern reader, but to the ancient Greeks, this would have been a reassuring safeguard for the future prosperity of their city. Within living memory, the Athenians had risen victoriously to the measure of their strength and vanquishing their enemies despite being outnumbered time and time again. This war became the defining feature

[39] Orrieux & Pantel 1995
[40] *3.15.7*

of the Athenian mindset, one that made them arrogant enough to steal the Delian treasury and presume their superiority over all others, including their bellicose neighbors, the Spartans.

Looking back, this seems an attitude more befitting Ares than Athena, a distinction that should have been apparent to the Athenian policymakers of the time. Athena was the goddess of war, wisdom, women at the loom, carpenters, charioteering, horse-taming, and shipbuilding. Walter Burket, a historian, remarked at how Athena had united all of these "divergent spheres of competence [not as an] elemental force, but [as] the force of civilization." He continued, "It is not the wild olive of Olympia, but the cultivated tree which is the fit of Athena. Poseidon violently sires the horse, Athena bridles it and builds the chariot; Poseidon excites the waves, Athena builds the ship; Hermes may multiply the flocks, Athena teaches the use of wool. Even in war Athena is no exponent of derring-do—this is captured in the figure of Ares—but cultivates the war-dance, tactics and discipline; when Odysseus, crafter and self-controlled as he is, persuades the Achaeans to join battle in spite of the war-weariness, then this is the work of Athena."[41]

Athena, then, was a civilizing ideal. It was on that ideal and its singular presence in Athens upon which the Athenians based their arrogance. This was not a belief held by Athenians alone; most "Hellenes" believed "Hellenic" culture—unified and established by the Pan-Hellenic sanctuaries and festivals such as Samothrace and the Olympic and Isthmian Games—was superior to any others, including the Egyptian, despite the fact that the Greeks always acknowledged its antiquity.

Even in the *Iliad*, Athena is never bested by mighty Ares. After Zeus prohibited the gods from taking part in the Trojan War, he relented, let them choose sides, and saw to the end of the bloodshed through definitive victory. Ares, however, was furious with Athena, and he sought out personal revenge before heeding Zeus' orders. "Wherefore now again, thou dog-fly, art thou making gods to clash with gods in strife, in the fierceness of thy daring, as thy proud spirit sets thee on? Rememberest thou not what time thou movedst Diomedes, Tydeus' son, to wound me, and thyself in the sight of all didst grasp the spear and let drive straight at me, and didst rend my fair flesh? Therefore shalt thou now methinks, pay the full price of all that thou hast wrought."[42] At this, he aimed his spear at Athena's breast but was knocked back when the blade hit the unyielding aegis she wore as her breastplate. Athena took a step back and found a boulder at her side which she lifted with ease and brought crashing down on stunned Ares's neck. Laughing, she admonished the god for his hubris: "Fool, not even yet hast thou learned how much mightier than thou I avow me to be, that thou matchest thy strength with mine. On this wise shalt thou satisfy to the full the Avengers invoked of thy mother, who in her wrath deviseth evil against thee, for that thou hast deserted the Achaeans and bearest aid to the overweening Trojans."[43]

---

[41] Burkert 1996
[42] *Homer Iliad 21.395*
[43] *Homer Iliad 21.410*

As Walter Burkert so succinctly put it, "Ares embodies everything that is hateful in war; the splendor of victory, Nike, is reserved for Athena."[44] In the temple of "Wingless Nike," Athena was worshipped there as Athena Nike, but her statue was a wooden cult statue (*Xoanon*) depicting her with a helmet in one hand and a pomegranate tree branch, symbolic of war and peace respectively. Ares, then, is the single-minded god of fighting, whereas Athena is capable of embodying war and peace when necessary.

Olympia was another Pan-Hellenic festival and possibly the most famous one after the oracular center of Delphi. In the 5th century BCE, it underwent huge architectural changes, including a new temple to Zeus, which housed the enormous chryselephantine statue of Zeus sitting inside, made of both gold and ivory. After their inauguration in 776 BCE, nearly all in the Greek poleis visited the sanctuary every four years to take part in the Olympian Games. When they visited, they brought various offerings—everything from statues to pottery, as far as the archaeological record reveals—to both Zeus and Hera for their blessings.

One such offering was a statue of Nike, made by the sculptor Paionios from Chalkidiki, dedicated around 425 BCE. The statue was made of the same Parian marble from which the Nike of Samothrace was sculpted, and as in the case of the Nike of Callimachus, the dedicatory inscription still survives. It reads, "The Messanians and the Naupaktians dedicated this statue to Zeus Olympios from the spoils of the wars. Paionios of Mende made it, who also won the competition to make the akroteria of the temple."[45]

---

[44] Burkert 1996
[45] See Museum of Classical Archaeology Database University of Cambridge Website

Carole Raddato's picture of the statue

It says the statue was dedicated by the Messanians and the Naupaktians, but historians believe the phrase "from the spoils of the wars" refers to the Peloponnesian War between Athens and Sparta. Given the time of its construction and dedication, the statue was most likely dedicated by the Athenians as well. Pausanias seems to agree with this conclusion in his writings about Olympia: "The Dorian Messenian who received Naupactus from the Athenians dedicated at Olympia the image of Victory upon the pillar. It is the work of Paeonius of Mende, and was made from the proceeds of enemy spoils, I think from the war with the Arcarnanians and Oeniadae. The Messenians themselves declare that their offering came from their exploit with the Athenians in the island of Sphacteria, and that the name of their enemy was omitted through dread of the Lacedaemonians; for, they say, they are not in the least afraid of Oeniadae and the Acarnanians."[46]

Ordinarily, the name of the defeated peoples would have been inscribed on a victory monument. Choosing not to include it on Paionios's statue "through dread of the Lacedaemonians (Spartans)," gives the reader a good idea of the state of the political climate at the time. The Peloponnesian War raged from ca. 431-404 BCE, placing the dedication of Nike at Olympia at the height of the war that would drag both the willing and unwilling poleis into it for the better part of the next 20 years. Even still, Nike deserved a celebration of her gifts, and this is what the Athenians and Messenians wished to give her, albeit hushed.

Pausanias describes other statues of Nike at Olympia, too, though that of Paionios is by far the most famous today. One of these statues stands as another example of the ancient Greeks' desire to "keep a god in one place": "Beside the Athena [statue at Olympia] has been set up a Nike. The Mantineans [of Arkadia] dedicated it, but they do not mention the ware in the inscription. Kalamis (Calamis) is said to have made it without wings in imitation of the wooden image at Athens called Nike Apteron (Wingless Victory)."[47]

Wingless Nike seems to have been a much-desired presence in the ancient Greek city, then. This gives rise to the idea that if she were left with her wings, she would alight the prow of some other polis's ship and bestow upon them her alluring charms.

Flitting and furtive though Nike may be, she is never tarred with the same capricious brush as that of other goddesses, such as Aphrodite, suffered in the mythological canon. Her "favors" were granted with the wisdom of the ineffable divine, a quality the figures of myth rarely succeed in achieving. Her presence in statue or bas-relief form bestowed this ineffability upon the god or goddess with whom she is associated, for instance, in the case of Athena in the Parthenon, and as described here by Pausanias again, Zeus at Olympia: "In his [the statue of Zeus in his temple at Olympia] right hand he carried a Nike, which, like the statue, is of ivory and gold; she wears a ribbon and—on her head—a garland...There are four Nikai (Nicae, Victories), represented as dancing women, one at each foot of the throne, and two others at the base of each foot."[48]

---

[46] 5.26.1
[47] 5. 26. 6 -7
[48] 5.11.1

The Odes

A 5th century BCE depiction of Nike

Marie Lan-Nguyen's picture of another 5th century BCE depiction of Nike

In the 5th century BCE, the renovations at Olympia took two forms. The first was that of extravagant, bombastic religious statues and temples, which abandoned the original temple to Zeus and Hera for two new and separate temples, one for each of the deities.[49] The stadium, too, was expanded to meet the surge of popularity the Olympic Games had acquired and the vast swathes of people they attracted to Olympia.[50] From the end of the 5th century BCE to the modern Olympic Games in Athens in 2004, Paionios's Nike has encapsulated the "Olympian" form of non-military victory. On the medals of the modern Athenian Olympic Games was etched the image of Paionios's Nike and a poem that read, "Mother of golden-crowned contests, *Olympia*, queen of truth!" The poem was written by the famed writer of victory odes, Pindar.

"Water is best, and gold, like a blazing fire in the night, stands out supreme of all lordly wealth. But if, my heart, you wish to sing of contests, look no further for any star warmer than the sun, shining by day through the lonely sky, and let us not proclaim any contest greater than Olympia. From there glorious song enfolds the wisdom of poets, so that they loudly sing the son of Cronus when they arrive at the rich and blessed hearth of Hieron, who wields the sceptre of law in Sicily of many flocks, reaping every excellence at its peak, and is glorified by the choicest music, which we men often play around his hospitable table. Come, take the Dorian lyre down from its peg, if the splendor of Pisa and of Pherenicus placed your mind under the influence of sweetest thoughts, when that horse ran swiftly beside the Alpheus, not needing to be spurred on in the race, and brought victory to his master, the king of Syracuse who delights in horses."[51] These are the first lines in Pindar's (c. 522 BC to c.443 BC) famous "Olympian Odes." The first of these odes is dedicated to "Hieron of Syracuse" who won the Single Horse Race in 476 BCE at the Olympic Games. These odes were referred to as "epinician"—from the Greek words "epi," meaning "around/upon/about," and "nike" in its mundane form—and they were the type of poetry at which Pindar excelled. Hieron of Syracuse would have commissioned the ode from Pindar in honor of his victory at the games, and he was certainly not the only one to do so.

Pindar's Odes were commissioned for victories at all of the Pan-Hellenic Games. Olympia, Corinth, Delphi, and Nemea hosted these games in alternating years, during which the elite of the ancient Greek poleis would partake and wish for their victories to be immortalized in song. Very often, Pindar entwined the story of the victor's homeland, familial connections, and even the actions and moments bringing about his victory. Such was the case of one Xenocrates of Acragas, who won the chariot race at the Isthmian Games in Corinth around 470 BCE: "But enough, for you are wise. I sing the Isthmian victory with horses, not unrecognized, which Poseidon granted to Xenocrates, and sent him a garland of Dorian wild celery for his hair, to have himself crowned, thus honouring the man of the fine chariot, the light of the people of Acragas. And in Crisa widely powerful Apollo looked graciously on him, and gave him glory there as well. And joined with the renowned favours of the sons of Erectheus in splendid Athens, he found no fault with the chariot-preserving hand of the man who drove his horses, the hand with which Nicomachus gave the horses full rein at the right moment—that driver whom the

[49] Whitely 2004
[50] ibid.
[51] Pindar Olympian 1

heralds of the seasons, the Elean truce-bearers of Zeus son of Cronus recognized, since they had no doubt experienced some hospitable act of friendship from him. And with sweet-breathing voice they greeted him when he fell into the lap of golden Victory in their own land, which they call the precinct of Olympian Zeus, where the sons of Aenesidamus were linked with immortal honours."[52]

"Falling into the lap of Victory" is indicative of the rhetorical beauty Pindar employed in his odes—the victor falls exhausted into Nike's lap and she comforts him, placing upon his head the wreath of glory he earned. This connection with the divine would not have been out of place at any of these sporting games because in each of the great cities hosting them, they formed part of a wider religious festival. The stadium in Olympia was expanded in the 4th century, which was part of a greater expansion of the religious areas, too. Eulogizing the feats of men by intertwining them with the works of the gods was the norm in the epinician poems.

I. Sailko's picture of pottery depicting Nike presenting a wreath

Victors commissioned odes expecting them to be personalized. This is a departure from the typical "prayer model" of most religious practices, but it was very in-keeping with ancient Greek religious practice. A large portion of religious festivals was dedicated to dance and choral song, but as Walter Burkert noted, "[T]he cult in no way demands the repetition of ancient, magically

---

[52] Isthmian 2.14-29

fixed hymns. On the contrary, the hymn must always delight the god afresh at the festival; therefore for the dance and hymn there must always be someone who makes it, the poet, *poietes*. The choral lyric, which can be traced from the end of the seventh century, accordingly develops from the practice of the cult and culminates in the first half of the fifth century in the work of Pindar."[53]

This is an important point to bear in mind when considering the role of Nike in ancient Greek mythology. She did more than just "embody" what soldiers and sportsmen desired most, and she was a goddess who could be supplicated or scorned not unlike any other. As a fragment of Simonides (translated by D. A. Campbell) shows, Nike was far from an abstract concept epinician—she chose the person upon whom she would bestow these honors: "[T]o win glory, stepping into the chariot of honoured Nike (Victory): for to one man only does the goddess grant to jump into her great carriage."[54] Her voice may have been hushed and her presence merely implied in the great Greek myths known to modern readers, but to the ancient Greeks, her silence was portentous, rather than insignificant.

Another writer of epinician odes, Bacchylides, whose works survive mostly in small fragments today, encapsulated the role of Nike at the Pan-Hellenic Games as follows: "Nike (Victory), giver of sweetness, to you the father, son of Ouranos (Uranus), on his high bench has granted glorious honour, so that in gold-rich Olympos you stand beside Zeus and judge the outcome of prowess for immortals and mortals: be gracious, daughter of thick-tressed, right-judging Styx; it is thanks to you that Metapontion…is now filled with the celebrtions and festivities of strong-limbed youths, and they sing the praises of the Pythian victor."[55] Far from an evocative image surrounding Zeus's statue at Olympia, then, Nike is shown here to be the goddess for whom the pilgrims to the Pan-Hellenic festivals raced and sang.

The role of the epinician odes was to both elucidate and build upon this mentality, and it was done with increasing skill over the years. Burkert explained that "the invocation of the gods, the enunciation of wishes and entreaties, is interwoven ever more artfully with mythical narratives and topical allusions to the festival and chorus. Already in the seventh century [BCE] several choruses are competing for the honour of performing the most beautiful hymn—with the costuming of the chorus then also playing its role. The religious function, the relationship with the gods, in in danger of being lost in the rivalry; but all are well convinced that the gods, like men, take a delighted interest in the contest."[56]

These odes were written with a three-fold design, the first of which was exaltation of the gods whose stories were intertwined with those of the victor's. The second two can be derived from this fragment from Bacchylides: "By the altar of Zeus, best ruler, the flowers of glory-bringing

---

[53] 1996
[54] 1982
[55] Fragment 11, see Campbell 1982
[56] 1996

Nike [i.e. the victory crown of the Games] nourish for men—a few mortals—a golden reputation conspicuous in their life-time always; and when the dark-blue cloud of death covers them there is left behind undying fame for the deed well done."[57]

Nike was capable of not only granting the victor "a golden reputation conspicuous in their lifetime always," but in fact, immortalizing them in as close a way as ever a mortal man could be. Thus, it is not unreasonable to suggest the writers of these epinician odes hoped to be "crowned" by Nike for their orations for the victors of the Games. Here is a rare example of Bacchylides doing exactly that: "Far-famed daughter of Pallas, lady Nike, may you always look with favor on the lovely chorus of the Karthaians (Carthaeans) the sons of Kranaus (Cranaus) and in the pastimes of the Mousai (Muses) crown Bakkhylides (Bacchylides) of Keos (Ceos) with many garlands."[58]

Coinage

Classical Numismatic Group, Inc.'s picture of an ancient coin depicting Nike

Coinage is an excellent resource for the modern historian. After coinage was invented in Lydia in the late 7th century BCE, it was adopted by the poleis of Greece to express their civic identity via stamps impressed onto the (usually) silver of which they were made. By the 5th century BCE, not only had most of the poleis adopted coinage, they had begun to mint their own (with the interesting exceptions of Sparta and Crete), and individuality was paramount among the minters. "No one could be in any doubt that a 'turtle' was Aeginetan, an 'owl' Athenian, and that an 'Arethousa' hailed from Syracuse. It is hard to resist the conclusion that coins were more

---

[57] Frag. 13. See Campbell 1992
[58] Epigrams 2

important as a badge of a city's identity and autonomy than as a medium for international exchange. [Coinage] remains a more a potent symbol of a political idea—the autonomous citizen-state."[59]

Coins became a source of rivalry among the poleis, not in the form of expressing a poleis's wealth, per se, but by demonstrating their artistic talent and commemorating victories. Nike is, therefore, one of the most common figures to appear on coinage, and her depictions are both impressive and multitudinous. There are examples of her forging trophies to give to victors of battles and games, hovering above horses, and crowning them with her garlands. In a later 4th century BCE feat of artistic dexterity, she is depicted nude to the waist, seemingly carving the name of the city onto the coin in which she appears.[60] She is also depicted crowning names of cities and people, as is the case in the 3rd century BCE coinage from Thrace, showing Lysimachos, one of Alexander the Great's generals, being crowned by a winged Nike standing in Athena's hands.

It seems that despite the fact cities minted coinage to maintain their identities, they could not resist depicting Nike as a familiar, emotive symbol. Instead—as is the case with the poetry and choral songs of the Pan-Hellenic religious festivals—the principal intention of the artisans making coinage stamps was to outdo their opponents by finding new and innovative ways of "delighting the goddess."

Conclusion

It is often presumed the purpose of these "abstract concept" deities was merely to give names to the myriad mysteries of the world. Harmonia, Phobos (fear), Hypnos (sleep), and of course, Thanatos (death) are characters whose names, not unlike that of Nike, make no attempt at veiling their roles in the cosmos. Unlike these other deities, however, Nike's role in ancient Greek thought is much more practical. She was invoked by warriors and bards, not in the same sense as a modern-day person hoping for victory might, but rather in a more conversational, interpersonal sense. She was often propitiated in extreme ways—as in the case of the "Wingless Nike" of Athens—and she was thanked, as any other deity would be.

Nike chose the person upon whom she would bestow victory, and she was an active participant of the activities of life, both real and mythic. In his *Dionysica*, the Hellenized Egyptian poet Nonnus, writing sometime in the 4th or 5th centuries CE, had Nike play an exceptionally important role when he wrote, "Nike (Victory) lifted her shield and held it before Zeus."[61] Even in the comedies of Aristophanes, Nike's name is deemed perfectly suitable to list immediately beside that of Hermes: "[On winged gods:] Hermes is a god and has wings and flies, and so do many other gods. First of all, Nike (Victory) flies with golden wings, Eros (Love) is undoubtedly

---

[59] Whitely 2004
[60] Sayles 2007
[61] 2.414

winged too, and Iris (Messenger) is compared by Homer to a timorous dove."[62]

Her association with Athena is so close that it nearly becomes symbiotic. Nike appears as the single voice of courage in the myth featuring Zeus and Typhon, in which Athena is often shown as either fleeing Mount Olympus with the other gods or voicing the words of Nike herself, yet her personality is often relegated to a mere epithet or "aspect" of the goddess of wisdom. To the ancient Greek, this would not have muted Nike's personality; instead, it would have contributed to and magnified Athena's aspects. An analysis of this symbiotic relationship appears in the Medieval Byzantine encyclopaedia, the *Souda*: "Nike Athena: Alternatively [she stands] allegorically for the notion that even winning is completely dependent on thought; for thought contributes to victory, but being thoughtless and impetuous while fighting leads to defeat. When she has wings she symbolizes that aspect of the mind that is sharp and, so to speak, swift-winged; but when she is depicted without wings she represents that aspect of it that is peaceful and quiet and civil, that by which the things of the earth flourish, a boon of which the pomegranate in her right hand is a representation. Just as the helmet in her left [is a representation] of battle. Thus she has the same capability as Athena."

Without the power for "thought," victory is not guaranteed, and for that reason, Nike is associated with Athena rather than Ares. It was this capacity for swift thought that influenced the artisans who carved her image into stone and the writers who invoked her powers in the epinician odes. "Victory" takes many forms, but the need for calm thought under pressure is one which inspirational writers and sports coaches continue to preach well into the 21st century. Nike is the representation of "victory," but in being so, she needs to embody characteristics that bring about victory, hence her connection with Athena, known as the wise strategist. According to the epinician odes, Nike bestows the final gift upon those who can demonstrate their similarity to her in their endeavours.

Whether singer, soldier, writer, or god, Nike is democratic in her gifts and only bestows them when she decides the effort has been completed to her satisfaction. In this way, she is both the template and the judge of victory. The 1st century (B)CE Roman writer, Ovid, captures the finality Nike brings to the victor in the contest between Athena and Poseidon for the dominion of Athens: "She shows an olive tree, springing pale-green with berries on the boughs; the gods admire; Victoria (Victory) [Nike] ends the work."[63]

Online Resources

Other books about ancient history by Charles River Editors

Other books about ancient Greece by Charles River Editors

---

[62] *Birds 574ff*
[63] 6. 82

Other books about Nike on Amazon

Bibliography

Atsma, A. J., (2017) *Theoi Project* Netherlands & New Zealand

Berens, E. M., (2007) *Myths and Legends of Greece and Rome* New York

Burkert, W., (1996) *Greek Religion* Blackwell Publishers

Campbell, J. (2008) *The Hero With A Thousand Faces* University of Princeton

Campbell, D. A., (1982) *Greek Lyric IV Bacchylides, Corinna, And Others* Loeb Classical Library Vol 461. Cambridge, Massachusetts: Harvard University Press.

Colavito, J., (2014) *Jason & The Argonauts Throughout The Ages* McFarland

Evelyn-White. H.G., (1914) *The Homeric Hymns and Homerica* Cambridge, MA. Harvard University Press

Frazer. J.G., (1921) *Apollodorus, The Library* Cambridge, MA, Harvard University Press

Fowler. H. N., (1925*) Plato Vol. 9* Cambridge, MA, Harvard University Press

Godley. A. D., (1920) *Herodotus Histories* Harvard University Press.

Graves, R., (1955) *The Greek Myths* Penguin

Hansen, W. F., (2004) *Handbook of Greek Mythology* Oxford University Press

Keesling, C., (2010). *"The Callimachus monument on the Athenian Acropolis (CEG 256) and Athenian Commemoration of the Persian Wars".* In Baumbach, Manuel; Petrovic, Andrej; Petrovic, Ivana. *Archaic and Classical Greek Epigram.* Cambridge University Press

Kirk, G. S., (1996) *Myth: Its Meaning And Function In Ancient And Other Cultures* University of California Press

Liddell, H.G., & Scott, R., (1940) *Greek-English Lexicon* Clarendon Press

Lindsay, J., ed. (1984) *Complete Plays of Aristophanes* Bantam Classics

Mallory. J.P and Adams. D.Q., (1997) *Encyclopaedia of Indo-European Culture*

Edited by J. P. Mallory, Douglas Q. Adams

Meyer. M. W., (1987) *The Ancient Mysteries: A Sourcebook* Harper Collins

Murray. A.T., (1924) *Homer's Iliad* Cambridge MA, Harvard University Press

Murray. A.T., (1919) *Homer's Odyssey* Cambridge MA, Harvard University Press

Ormerod. H.A. and Jones. W.H.S. (1918) *Pausanias Description of Greece* Cambridge MA, Harvard University Press

Orrieux, C. & Schmitt Pantel. P., (1995) *A History of Ancient Greece* Blackwell Publishing Ltd

Parker, R., (2007) *Polytheism and Society in Athens* Oxford University Press

Rieu, E.V., (1959) *The Argonautica of Apollonius of Rhodes* Penguin

Rouse, W.H.D., (1940) Nonnos *Dionysiaca* Loeb Classical Library. Cambridge, Massachusetts: Harvard University Press

Ruck. C.P and Staples. D., (2001) *The World of Classical Myth: Gods and Goddesses, Heroines and Heroes* Carolina Academic Press

Sayles, W., (2007) *Ancient Coin Collecting II: Numismatic Art of the Greek World* F+W Publications

Schmidt, L., (1882) *Die Ethik der altern Griechen* Hertz

Seaton, R. C., (1912) *Apollonius Rhodius Argonautica* Loeb Classical Library

Stewart, A., (2016), *The Nike of Samothrace: Another View* American Journal of Archaeology Vol. 120, No. 3 pp. 399-410

Svarlien, D.A., (1990) *Pindar: Odes* Yale University Press

Taylor, T., (1987) *The Orphic Hymns* Philosophical Research Society

Vernant, J. P., (1996) *Myth and Society in Ancient Greece* Zone Books

Vernant, J. P., (2006) *Myth and Thought in Ancient Greece* Zone Books

Vernant, J. P., (1982) *The Origins of Greek Thought* Cornell University Press

Way, A.S., (1913) *Quintus Smyrnaeus: The Fall of Troy* Loeb Classical Library

Whitely, J., (2004) *The Archaeology Of Ancient Greece* Cambridge

Free Books by Charles River Editors

We have brand new titles available for free most days of the week. To see which of our titles are currently free, click on this link.

Discounted Books by Charles River Editors

We have titles at a discount price of just 99 cents everyday. To see which of our titles are currently 99 cents, click on this link.

Made in the USA
Las Vegas, NV
27 February 2023

68248347R00036